Learning About Life Cycles

The Life Cycle of an

Oak Tree

Ruth Thomson

PowerKiDS
press.

New York

Published in 2009 by The Rosen Publishing Group Inc.
29 East 21st Street, New York, NY 10010

First Edition

Editor: Victoria Brooker
Designer: Simon Morse
Consultant: Michael Scott OBE, B.Sc

Library of Congress Cataloging-in-Publication Data

Thomson, Ruth, 1949-
    The life cycle of an oak tree / Ruth Thomson. — 1st ed.
        p. cm. — (Learning about life cycles)
    Includes index.
    ISBN 978-1-4358-2838-4 (library binding) —
    ISBN 978-1-4358-2888-9 (paperback)
    ISBN 978-1-4358-2894-0 (6-pack)
    1. Oak—Life cycles—Juvenile literature. I. Title. II. Series:
Thomson, Ruth, 1949- Learning about life cycles
(PowerKids Press)
    QK495.F14T46 2009
    583'.46—dc22

                                        2008025783

Manufactured in China

Photographs: Cover (main) Nigel Cattin/Holt Studios
International Ltd/Alamy; 2, 7 Derek Croucher/Alamy; 22
Bart Elder/Alamy; 4-5 Edward Parker/Alamy; Cover (tr, cr,
br) 6, 8, 9, 10, 11, 12, 13, 14, 15, 16, 17, 18, 19, 20, 21, 23
(all) naturepl.com

Web Sites

Due to the changing nature of
Internet links, PowerKids Press has
developed an online list of Web sites
related to the subject of this book.
This site is updated regularly.
Please use this link to access this list:
www.powerkidslinks.com/lalc/oak

Contents

Oak trees grow here

Oak trees grow in woods, parks, and the countryside. In woods, oak trees grow tall to reach the sunlight. In the open, their branches spread out wide.

What is an oak tree?

An oak tree has **broad**, soft leaves and rough **bark** on its trunk. Its branches spread both up and outward.

stalk

oak leaf

crown

Bark protects the tree from drying out and insect attack.

branch

trunk

All oak trees produce hard nuts, called acorns, that sit in a cup. Inside every acorn is a **seed** that could grow into a new oak tree.

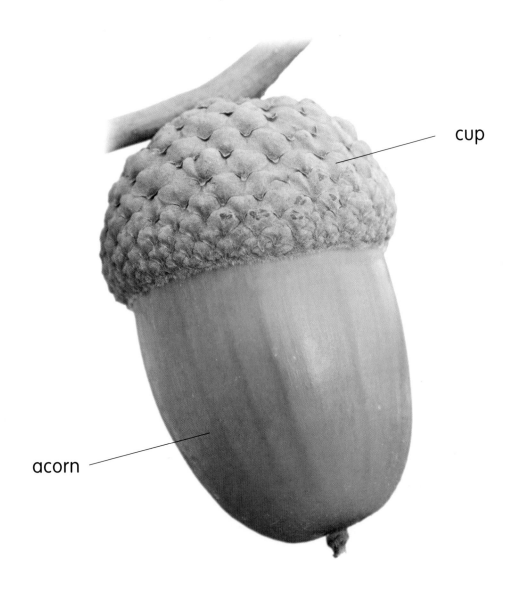

cup

acorn

Acorns

In the fall, acorns drop to the ground. Most land in places where they cannot grow. Deer or birds eat many of them. Squirrels bury some to eat in the winter.

In the spring, buried acorns soak
up water from the soil. They swell
and their shell splits. A **root** starts
growing down into the soil.

Shoots

A small **shoot**
pushes out of the soil
and reaches upward
to the sunlight.
Two small **seed**
leaves unfold.

The shoot keeps growing.
By the end of the summer,
it has about six new leaves.

6 months

Sapling

Oak trees grow slowly. The young tree is called a sapling. Every year it grows taller. Its **trunk** grows thicker. Twigs grow from the trunk.

5 years

The twigs grow longer and thicker and become branches. More and more leaves appear. **Roots** grow deeper and spread wider, too.

20 years

Tree

The tree is now a well-grown adult. Its roots take up water, which travels up the trunk to the leaves. Leaves use air and sunlight to make food for the tree.

In the fall, there is not enough
light for leaves to make food.
The leaves change color,
die, and fall off the tree.

Winter buds

The bare tree rests all winter, while the weather is cold and windy, and there is less light.

Leaves and flowers start to grow
on the tip of each twig. They stay
tightly closed in the winter. Before
these open, they are called buds.

Flowers

In the spring, buds open into leaves and flowers. There are male and female flowers. The hanging male flowers are called catkins. These are full of **pollen**.

Wind blows the pollen onto the female flowers of another oak tree. These will grow into acorns. By September, the acorns are fully grown.

Old trees

Oak trees can live for hundreds of years. Every year, new leaves, flowers, and acorns appear. The **trunk** grows wider and the branches grow longer.

500 years

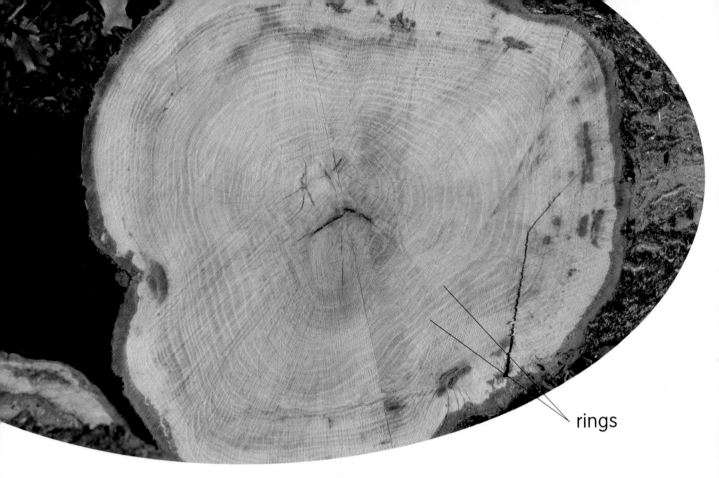

rings

Tree stumps

Sometimes, trees die of disease.
Many are cut down. If you count
the rings on a tree stump, you
can tell how old the tree was.